BUSINESS PORTRAITS

McDONALD'S

Published by VGM Career Horizons,
a division of NTC Publishing Group,
4255 West Touhy Avenue
Lincolnwood (Chicago), Illinois 60646-1975, U.S.A.

J338.7
GOUL

Gould, William, 1947–
    VGM's business portraits: McDonald's/William Gould.
        p. cm. – (VGM's business portraits)
    Includes index.
    ISBN 0-8442-4778-2 (alk. paper)
    1. McDonald's Corporation – Juvenile literature. 2. Fast food
restaurants – United States – Juvenile literature. I. Title.
II. Series.
TX945.5.M33G68 1996
338.7'6164795'73-dc20   96-10230
                                                            CIP
                                                            AC

Manufactured in the United Kingdom.

BUSINESS PORTRAITS

McDONALD'S

WILLIAM GOULD

VGM Career Horizons
a division of *NTC Publishing Group*
Lincolnwood, Illinois USA

ACKNOWLEDGMENT

Our thanks to The McDonald's Corporation for providing us with copies of their annual reports and historical publications from which we drew information to develop a profile of the company. Editorial comments made and conclusions reached by the author about general business practices of international companies do not necessarily reflect the policies and practices of The McDonald's Corporation.

Our thanks also to Burger King and PepsiCo for supplying us with photographs and permission to use their logos; and to Mike Atkinson, Malcolm Porter, Neil Reed and John York for their illustrations.

CONTENTS

■ People

■ Things

■ Money

▲ Businesses need people (human resources), things (physical resources) and money (capital).

▼ A business uses money to buy human and physical resources, and create a product or service which it sells for a profit.

The adventure of business

Business often sounds difficult but its basic principles are simple, and it can be very exciting. The people involved in the creation and running of the businesses we examine in VGM'S BUSINESS PORTRAITS faced challenges and took risks that make some adventure stories seem dull.

What is a business?

If you sell a spare book or banana to your friend for money you are making a business deal. Anyone who produces goods or services in return for money, or works for an organization that does so, is involved in business.

Businesses try to make profits. They try to sell things for more than the amount the things cost them to make. They usually invest part of the profit they make to produce and sell more of their products. If they have no money to invest, they may borrow it.

The language of business

Many of the technical terms that make the language of business sound complicated are explained on pages 46 and 47.

Business matters

Yellow panels throughout the book explain general business concepts. Blue panels tell you more about McDonald's.

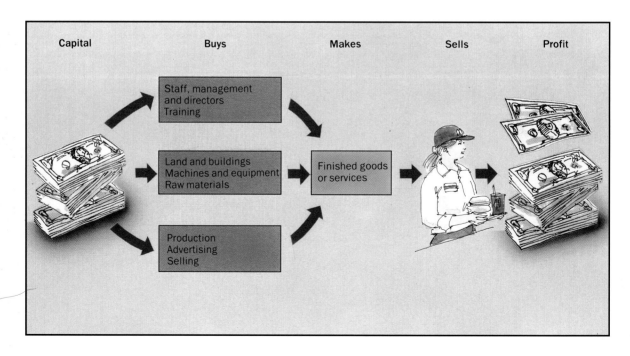

Capital   Buys   Makes   Sells   Profit

Staff, management and directors
Training

Land and buildings
Machines and equipment
Raw materials

Finished goods or services

Production
Advertising
Selling

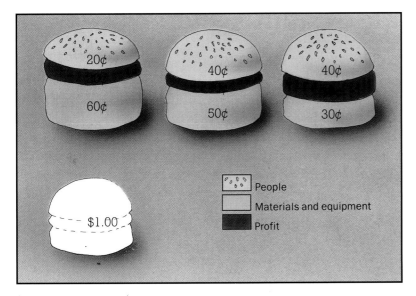

The purpose of a business is to make a profit. Profit is the amount of money earned from sales that remains after all the costs are paid. If a burger sells for one dollar and costs 70 cents to make and sell, the profit is 30 cents.

People
Materials and equipment
Profit

The McDonald's adventure

McDonald's sells more hamburgers than any other company. Its Golden Arches symbol can be seen in the heart of virtually every major city and many, many smaller ones. Against aggressive competition from other fast-food companies, McDonald's has continued to grow, and shows no sign of slowing down. Every day food and drink are supplied to more than 28 million people, and all around the world new McDonald's restaurants open their doors to eager customers.

▲ Even if they can't read Russian, there are few people in the western world who could not translate the name on this poster. McDonald's Big Mac, here being launched in Moscow, is one of the world's most famous food products.

◀ Crowds gather at McDonald's restaurant in Shenzhen, China, which opened in 1990.

McDonald's success

McDonald's is the best-known symbol of the fast-moving quick-service food industry. Since it was founded in the 1950s, it has become the largest hamburger restaurant chain in the world and is still growing. It is the fourth largest retailer in the United States. It employs half a million people there and hundreds of thousands more elsewhere. Its annual sales total more than $25 billion. One out of every six visits to a restaurant in the United States is said to be to a McDonald's.

Guiding principles

What makes McDonald's the success it is? How has it built such a stable business in an industry in which so many companies spring up and fail after a short time? Part of its success must result from its four guiding principles: quality, service, cleanliness and value (QSC&V to McDonald's staff). McDonald's sells high-quality, hygienically prepared food at affordable prices, and gives speedy and courteous service.

Suppliers

Many businesses depend on McDonald's as their major or only client. These companies supply meat, potatoes, baked products, soft drinks and so on to McDonald's. By insisting on quality from these suppliers, McDonald's has raised standards throughout the food-processing industry.

▲ McDonald's prides itself on the quality of its product. A Big Mac beef patty contains no additives, fillers, binders, preservatives or flavor enhancers – just pure beef.

▲ McDonald's counter crews offer fast, smiling service.

▲ McDonald's restaurants are cleaned continuously.

▶ McDonald's adds value by giving customers fun as well as food.

Some companies are profitable because they sell extremely expensive products to a few people who can afford them. Others are successful because they sell to ordinary people – the mass market – at a price everyone can afford. McDonald's self-service system would not have been a success if it had not enabled the company to sell its hamburgers at a price that would attract large numbers of people.

FACTS ABOUT McDONALD'S

* Largest quick-service food company in the world
* Second most recognized brand in the world
* Sales of nearly $26 billion in 1994 ($14.9 billion in the United States, $11 billion elsewhere)
* Profits of $2.2 billion in 1994
* Fourth largest retailer in the United States
* Serves 28 million people a day worldwide
* Headquarters is in Oak Brook, Illinois, a suburb of Chicago
* 17,000 outlets in 86 countries
* Employs 600,000 people worldwide including franchisees
* Has assets of $13.6 billion
* Opened in Moscow in 1990
* Has given more than $80 million to children's charities

▲ McDonald's seeks maximum publicity for its good works. Here Princess Diana is entertained by the company prior to presenting Child of Achievement awards.

▶ Over 70% of McDonald's packaging is made of recycled materials.

▼ McDonald's does not like to look out of place. Its restaurant in Shakespeare's Stratford-upon-Avon has "olde worlde" charm.

Quick service to self service

The fast-food industry began in the 1920s. Certain restaurants in the United States began serving food at the curbside to customers in their cars. Drive-in restaurants followed, where customers pulled in to a parking lot and waiters called carhops served them.

The McDonald brothers

Mac and Dick McDonald, who gave their name to the McDonald's chain, became part of this food revolution in 1940. They opened a restaurant in San Bernardino, California, a small town near Los Angeles. The building was eight-sided with the kitchen on view. From there 20 carhops delivered the 25 items on the menu. The drive-in was a huge success with teenagers.

▲ Mac (left) and Dick McDonald had no greater ambition than to live comfortably. They had no interest in running a nationwide, let alone a worldwide, business.

THE McDONALD BROTHERS

Maurice and Richard (Mac and Dick) McDonald moved to California from the eastern state of New Hampshire in 1930 to look for work. Many people, including their father, had been thrown out of work during the Great Depression. The two young men had gone west to make their fortune. After trying various jobs in Hollywood's developing film industry, they opened their first drive-in restaurant near Pasadena in 1937. It was a hot-dog stand, built with borrowed timber. Three years later, they had made enough money to open the San Bernardino restaurant – which they continued to run until 1961.

BUSINESS MATTERS: CAPITAL

To start up a business you need money – financial capital. If you are not wealthy you have to earn the money or borrow it. If you borrow it, you have to offer the lender something in return, usually a share in the business or interest on the money. The McDonald brothers saved the money they needed to start their first business and used the profits from the hot-dog stand to start their restaurant. They were successful enough never to have to borrow money.

By 1948 the McDonalds were wealthy but other drive-ins were giving them uncomfortable competition. They kept on losing carhops to competitors who paid more. They needed to provide a speedier service to make more sales. They also wanted to attract families.

Cuts and more cuts

One way to speed things up was to reduce the menu. They cut it to just nine items: hamburger (80% of orders included hamburgers), cheeseburger, potato chips, three types of soft drink, milk, coffee and a slice of pie. Later they added French fries and milkshakes to make 11 items.

The most important cut was the carhops. They fired them all. From now on, the restaurant was to be a take-out, a self-service carry-out. Customers ordered and collected their

food at a service window. It came in paper wrappers, bags and cups. With no china to be washed (broken or stolen), the brothers were also able to get rid of the dishwasher.

Change for the better

The McDonalds could now serve each customer more quickly and so serve many more people. But initially there were not more people. The teenagers missed the carhops and began to go elsewhere. The absence of the teenagers, however, made the restaurant more attractive to families, and sales began to pick up. The savings the McDonalds had made in labor costs and the increased turnover allowed them to charge less for the food — and still make a profit. The 15-cent hamburger had arrived, and so had the children and families who have remained the mainstay of McDonald's.

BUSINESS MATTERS: CHOICE

"If we gave people a choice," Dick McDonald said, "there would be chaos." A limited menu meant that fewer jobs had to be performed which meant that each customer's order could be filled more speedily and more cheaply. More people could be served so that, even though prices were lowered, the volume of sales would be higher. Henry Ford had used the same idea when he introduced the Model-T car, the first car to sell to the mass market. He said, "You can have any color you like, so long as it is black." There was no choice, but the car, produced on an assembly line, was cheap enough for ordinary people to buy. When people have more money at their disposal they can afford a choice. Nowadays people would not be satisfied with a small menu or a single style of car. Customers like to have a choice.

Mass production

By 1949 the San Bernardino restaurant had become a hamburger assembly plant. A 12-man crew (women were not employed) worked in the kitchen, each person carrying out one specific task. Grill men grilled hamburgers. Fry men cooked French fries. Dressers applied ketchup and mustard, and wrapped the burgers ready to go. Shake men mixed milkshakes. Countermen served customers. It worked like a factory assembly line.

Copying the McDonalds

Long lines formed at McDonald's during peak periods. By the mid-1950s, annual sales totalled $350,000. Other fast-food operators were keen to learn the McDonalds' secret.

Mac and Dick began to license their operation as the Speedy Service System in 1952. Neil Fox of Phoenix, Arizona, became their first licensee in 1953. He received a blueprint of the new building that the McDonalds designed and built for him, a week-long loan of one of the San Bernardino staff to show him the ropes, a basic description of the Speedy Service System in a slim manual, and the right to call his restaurant McDonald's – all for a single payment of $1,000. After that, he was on his own. The McDonalds had no further financial or business interest in him.

▲ This all-male crew from one of the earliest drive-ins in California worked with military precision and discipline. Each man was trained to do one job only.

▼ The San Bernardino restaurant in 1949, proudly announcing the 15-cent hamburger.

◀ Crews at a McDonald's restaurant today have more interesting and varied tasks than their counterparts in the early days of McDonald's.

Enough is enough

The McDonalds' casual approach to granting licenses showed how uninterested they were in developing the business. They were splitting annual profits of $100,000 a year. They lived together in a lavish 20-room mansion and treated themselves to a Cadillac car each once a year. Their pleasures were simple: they loved dining out in other people's restaurants and watching boxing matches.

The McDonalds seemed to fear making too much money. They worried about getting into the clutches of the taxman. When someone offered them $15,000 for a license to operate six McDonald's in Sacramento, they turned the offer down. They had invented a revolutionary fast-food system that appealed greatly to the American people, but they lacked the desire to develop it. The job of making McDonald's what it now is fell to a man of vision named Ray Kroc.

▲ Ray Kroc invented nothing; his brilliance lay in turning McDonald's into a multi-billion-dollar business.

RAY A. KROC, 1902-1984

Raymond Albert Kroc was born in Chicago in 1902. In 1917, when the United States entered World War I, he lied about his age and became a Red Cross ambulance driver at 15. After the war he made his living as a jazz pianist by night and as a paper-cup salesman by day. He also spent a year selling real estate (property and land). In 1939 he set up a company later called Prince Castle Sales Division Inc to sell the Multimixer milkshake machine nationwide. Kroc was 52 years old when he signed his contract with the McDonald brothers. Under it he set up McDonald's Corporation in 1955. He served as its chairman until 1977, and remained its guiding spirit until his death in 1984.

Selling the system

In the mid-1950s Ray A. Kroc was a middle-aged Chicago-based salesman with some 30 years' experience in selling supplies to the food service industry. He owned the exclusive right to market the Multimixer milkshake machine throughout the United States. Sales of the Multimixer were falling at the time, partly because of competition from a rival firm. But one of Kroc's customers – the McDonald's drive-in in San Bernardino – owned no less than eight Multimixers and in 1954 ordered two more. What could they be doing with them all?

Kroc flew to California and spent two days watching the drive-in to find out. Seeing the long lines of customers waiting for their burgers, fries and shakes, he got his answer. The brothers had an excellent product of consistently high quality (he particularly admired the French fries) and a brilliant operation that could be exploited nationwide. He went into the restaurant and made friends with the brothers.

Franchises

Between 1952 and 1954 the McDonald brothers sold only 15 franchises to operators wishing to use their system. They were happy to let people use it, but they wanted them to do it properly, especially if the outlets were to be called

BUSINESS MATTERS: FRANCHISING

Many large companies operate through a system of franchises. They grant a license to an individual or company (the franchisee, or licensee) to sell their goods or services. Franchising allows the franchiser (the organization granting the franchises) to control the franchisees' manufacturing or operating methods and the quality of their products. They may provide equipment, training and other services to their franchisees. In return, the franchisees get the benefit of the franchiser's name and reputation which will attract customers. Organizations that use franchising in various forms include KFC, Pizza Hut, Holiday Inn, Coca-Cola and the Ford Motor Company.

▲ KFC Express, Pizza Express and Taco Bell are all franchises licensed by PepsiCo. Together they are nearly twice the size of McDonald's.

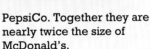

◀ Above average sales of this Multimixer milkshake machine to the McDonald brothers aroused Ray Kroc's curiosity. He recognized immediately that the Speedy-Service System was a business opportunity not to be missed.

McDonald's. The franchisees were expected to follow the way the McDonalds did things to the letter. But, alas, the McDonalds had no way of keeping their franchisees in line.

After paying their fee, the franchisees could change the way they operated if they wanted to. Many did. Some changed the menu, and at least one changed the name. Standards of hygiene and food quality dropped. There were also plenty of operators copying the McDonalds by just going to San Bernardino and watching them at work.

The franchising agent
Mac and Dick did not want the bother of selling and controlling franchises. They had tried to hire an agent to do it for them, but had failed. Then they met Ray Kroc. A week after his first visit, he flew back to San Bernardino to sign a contract as the new agent.

Efficiency helps a business run smoothly, effectively and profitably. Efficiency begins with developing ways of working that are easy to understand and do not waste time or energy. Division of labor, in which each worker carries out a specific job, increases speed. When you perform a task over and over again, you become very quick at it. You also become bored, however, so you need frequent breaks or a change of task. Simple jobs tend to be low-paid and unsatisfying, so people frequently stay in them only a short time, unless there are compensations, such as bonuses and a good working atmosphere, to motivate them. Constantly training new staff is inefficient, so companies like McDonald's try to keep their staff.

▶ Ray Kroc opened his first restaurant in Des Plaines, Illinois, in 1955. The price of a hamburger was still 15 cents. The restaurant is now a McDonald's museum.

Franchising in action

Under his contract with Mac and Dick, Ray Kroc had exclusive rights to sell their franchises all over the United States. By 1960 his company had become McDonald's Corporation, with a chain of 228 restaurants and total sales of $37.8 million.

Kroc himself became the first franchisee under the system. On 15 April 1955 he opened his own unit in Des Plaines, Illinois, a suburb of Chicago. It became the perfect McDonald's drive-in and one of the most successful.

Finding franchisees

To recruit his first operators, Kroc turned to friends at the golf club. He simply showed them the sales figures at his Des Plaines unit and they were eager to sign up. Some 18 of them bought franchises. The problem was that they did not need

the business. Most of them already owned a successful business and ran their McDonald's as a sideline. Standards soon began to fall.

Kroc realized that McDonald's needed franchisees who would dedicate themselves to their restaurants, people who would depend on the business for their sole livelihood. This type of franchisee was not rich, did not own a business and had usually given up another job to go into business alone. Such franchisees would work long hours to make their McDonald's a success.

▲ Not all McDonald's outlets are franchises. This glamorous restaurant, located in an airport terminal, is run directly by the company.

◄ Franchisee Mike Charles gave up a successful job, sold his property and used his savings to undertake his training at McDonald's. The risk paid off, and he now runs a rewarding restaurant.

Running a McDonald's today

If you take out a McDonald's franchise today, you have to pay a starting fee of more than $65,000. For this fee you receive the right to run one restaurant for 20 years. McDonald's buys or leases the site or premises of your restaurant; you pay the rent and a service fee. You hire and pay the staff. You also have to buy the specially designed equipment, the furniture and McDonald's signage. And of course you must buy the food – from approved McDonald's suppliers. In return you get training and support from its managers and extensive advertising. To make sure that you keep to the basics of the system, McDonald's supervisors will inspect and grade your restaurant regularly.

The buyout

For the franchisee, a McDonald's franchise could be a goldmine. But for Kroc's company the franchises were anything but profitable. If a franchisee had sales of $100,000, he might make a profit of $20,000. Of that only $1,400 would go to McDonald's. Kroc could not build his chain on so low an income.

Building capital

In 1956 Kroc hired Harry Sonneborn as McDonald's financial director. Sonneborn found a way of increasing the company's profits. He leased sites from landowners willing to build McDonald's units, and the company sublet the units to franchisees at a decent profit.

Sonneborn's property deals helped to build up McDonald's capital. As time went on, McDonald's began to buy rather than lease its units. It now owns so many that it has become one of the world's largest owners of retail property.

▲ Harry Sonneborn brought prosperity to McDonald's with his property deals. He thought that property would be a better longterm business than hamburgers. But the idea did not appeal to Ray Kroc, and Sonneborn left the business.

▲ Here we grow again! Ray Kroc and Fred Turner inspect the plans for yet another new restaurant.

▼ Where possible, McDonald's likes to own the freehold to its buildings, but it is not interested in making money out of property alone. This beautiful building is Denton House on Long Island, New York. It houses McDonald's 12,000th restaurant.

Buying out the brothers

During his first six years, Ray Kroc became increasingly frustrated with Mac and Dick McDonald. Every time he wanted to make even minor improvements to the system, Kroc had to seek their permission. But often they were not interested. They were happy living on their San Bernardino profits and the 0.5 per cent they made from Kroc's franchisees.

Kroc wanted full control of the system. In 1961 he asked the brothers how much they wanted for the rights to the system and the McDonald's name. Their price – $2,700,000 in cash – stunned him. Mac and Dick had carefully worked it out: $1 million each, plus $700,000 for the taxman. It was not a high price by modern standards, but for a struggling young company it was an enormous amount to raise.

Raising cash

Now Harry Sonneborn's property deals came into their own. Because the company owned property, it was able to raise the money. The property was security for the loan. The annual loan repayments were fixed at 0.5 per cent of McDonald's food sales – just what the company had been paying Mac and Dick. By the end of the year, the buyout was complete. Kroc was in control.

19

Going public

Today McDonald's is one of the largest corporations in the United States. It is a public company owned by its shareholders – banks, insurance companies and other financial institutions, directors and employees of McDonald's, and members of the public. But in the beginning it was owned by Ray Kroc alone.

The stock offer

In the late 1950s, Kroc was not making enough money to pay even key employees large salaries. Instead he gave company stock to senior members of staff. He himself had 52.7 per cent of McDonald's, giving him control of the company. Harry Sonneberg had 17.2 per cent, Kroc's secretary, June Martino, 7.6 per cent. The remaining 22.5 per cent was owned by two insurance firms that had helped obtain loans for McDonald's.

By 1965 McDonald's was a medium-sized corporation. Kroc and the other shareholders were ready to reap some of their rewards by selling some of their valuable stock. The company was also ready to build up its capital by going public – offering shares for sale to outsiders.

▲ Ray Kroc was keen to change the low-quality image projected by the company logo. He did away with "Speedee" the fast little chef and introduced a new design based on the arches and sloping roof of the typical restaurant. The arches crossed to form an M.

BUSINESS MATTERS: STOCKS AND SHARES

A company's stock is its total capital. This includes the money that it earns and its assets, the properties and other things that it owns. When a company goes public it sells all or part of its stock, in the form of shares, to the public. Shares are just what they sound like – a share of the company. People buy and sell shares on the stock market. They hope to buy shares at a low price and sell them when they increase in value. Their value will increase if the company does well, but fall if it does badly. Like entrepreneurs, people who buy stocks and shares – investors – take a risk in the hope of making a good investment. They need to be good at spotting companies that will do well in the future.

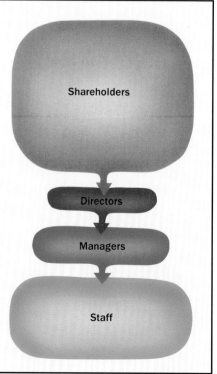

► A public company like McDonald's is owned by its shareholders. The board of directors is answerable to them. The management and staff are answerable to the board.

A good prospect

McDonald's was a good bet for the stock market. It had 700 restaurants and five regional offices spread throughout the states, as well as a large property empire. When its stock went on sale on April 15, 1965, there was a rush to buy shares. With more buyers than there were shares, the price per share rose from $22.50 to $30 on the first day of trading. Within weeks they were $49. Kroc, Sonneberg and Martino were all millionaires.

WOMEN AT WORK

Throughout the 1950s and early 1960s, McDonald's refused to employ women as crew members or counter staff. They feared that women might flirt with their male colleagues or attract the wrong type of customer to a family restaurant! But in the mid-1960s, a time of low unemployment in the United States, when men were not always available to fill job vacancies, McDonald's franchisees broke the rule and began hiring women. The men-only rule was formally abandoned in 1968. Now many of McDonald's best managers are women.

WHAT HAPPENED TO MAC AND DICK?

After selling their system to Ray Kroc, the McDonald brothers handed their San Bernardino drive-in over to two long-time employees and retired. Mac died in 1971. Dick went to live in New Hampshire, his home state. In 1962 Kroc opened a McDonald's unit in San Bernardino, not far from the original McDonald's drive-in, which had to be renamed the Big M. The new unit's purpose was to put the Big M out of business, and it succeeded. Sales at the Big M plunged. In 1968 it changed hands, and in 1970 it closed.

Freedom and choice

Anyone who becomes a McDonald's franchisee must follow the rules for operating the system laid out in the manual. The manual provides a step-by-step guide to ordering supplies, checking their quality, storing and cooking products, and reporting problems. The franchisee must obtain everything his or her restaurant needs from suppliers approved by McDonald's. All franchisees must observe McDonald's very strict codes on quality, cleanliness, service and value.

Franchisees' freedom?

Back in the 1940s the McDonald brothers speeded up their service by limiting the items offered. Nowadays McDonald's can maintain its speed of service while giving its customers a wider choice. Most of the ideas for new items on the menu come from franchisees. They are closer to their customers and know what they want.

▲ Jim Delligati, a franchisee from Pittsburgh, Pennsylvania, persuaded the company to let him test a double-decker burger in 1967. It became the Big Mac and was introduced nationwide the following year.

CUSTOMERS' CHOICE

These are some of the products that have been introduced in specific countries around the world.

* Filet-O-Fish Sandwich (US)
* Egg McMuffin (US)
* Big Mac (US)
* Chicken McNuggets (US)
* Chicken Sandwich (US)
* Vegetable McNuggets (UK)
* Salads (UK)
* Pizzas (UK)
* Vegetable Burger (Netherlands)
* McLax (Norway)
* McNoodles (Hong Kong)
* Kosher meat (Israel)
* Beer (Germany)
* Burritos (US)

Big Mac

French Fries

Chicken McNuggets

Before introducing new items, franchisees must get approval from McDonald's. This can take time. Every new item has to undergo rigorous market testing. In the 1960s Ray Kroc tried several times to introduce a dessert but failed each time. He could not find one that appealed to enough people or could be fitted into the assembly-line preparation methods. It was a franchisee who came up with the apple pie that is now a standard item on the menu.

Customers' choice

Successful new products fill a particular need. The first addition to the McDonald's menu came in 1962. Lou Groen, a franchisee in Cincinnati, Ohio, found that business was slack on Fridays. Many of his customers were Roman Catholics who at that time were not allowed to eat meat on Fridays. His answer was to develop a fish sandwich. The new item proved popular in tests – and not just on Fridays – and took its place on the McDonald's menu nationwide as the Filet-O-Fish Sandwich.

▲ McDonald's offers more and more choices for breakfast as more and more people eat breakfast out rather than at home.

Filet-O-Fish

Bacon & Egg McMuffin

Apple Pie

▼ McDonald's immense purchasing power enables it to purchase ingredients of uniformly high quality.

The product

Food sold in the United States has to comply with regulations made by the Food and Drug Administration (FDA). Similar government bodies operate food laws in other countries. Many people have criticized fast food in general as junk food low in nutritional value. But independent experts maintain that a typical meal of burger, fries and a shake contains most of the key nutrients a person needs every day. Unfortunately, it also contains a high proportion of fat, though the fat content in a McDonald's meal is now almost a third less than it was. McDonald's has also introduced items that contain fewer calories in response to a demand for less fattening foods, especially for young people. In many McDonald's you can now buy a low-calorie meal of broiled chicken, salad and diet Coke.

Quality control

Qualified food technologists at laboratories in McDonald's headquarters carry out exhaustive quality tests on all the food products that the company uses. They inspect food with microscopes and chemically analyse samples. They provide a 50-item test that helps franchisees check that their meat supplies are sound. Customers know that the cattle for McDonald's beef are fed on grain and killed humanely.

Like most large food retailers McDonald's cannot risk releasing inferior produce on to the market. No matter how large or important McDonald's suppliers are, they know that if their performance slips McDonald's will go elsewhere. They try always to be ready for the unannounced visits of McDonald's testers and tasters. McDonald's does its best to help suppliers and managers reach standards that are well above government regulations.

◀ Testing buns in the bakery. McDonald's suppliers know that, if one quality check is failed, the whole consignment of a product will be rejected.

▼ McDonald's delivery vehicles are multi-temperature and carry all types of goods.

BUSINESS MATTERS: SERVING THE SERVERS

A regular supply of goods and services of consistent quality is crucial to most businesses. Large companies often make certain of essential supplies by buying a controlling interest in companies that provide them. Before McDonald's gave them its business, most of its suppliers were small companies; now many are among the largest food-service companies in the United States and elsewhere. For all of them McDonald's is their main or sole customer.

McDonald's did not set out to use small suppliers. In its early days, the company simply could not get credit from established large-scale hamburger meat processors, so it had to go to smaller suppliers. These smaller companies were keen to meet McDonald's exacting demands, sometimes risking everything to get the business.

Putting on the style

If you walk or drive into a McDonald's anywhere in the world, you will find much the same things. The Golden Arches beckon you in. A typical restaurant is a sturdy building with a tiled floor and lots of tables with rounded corners and comfortable seating. At one end is a wide counter, and above it the brightly lit menu in both words and pictures. Behind the counter, McDonald's kitchen crew can be seen hard at work.

The effect is clean, bright and full of light. The counter staff in their fresh uniforms are trained to process your order quickly and courteously. The atmosphere is friendly. In some restaurants there are toys and play areas. McDonald's knows that it has a special appeal for children.

▲ The Golden Arches symbol is one of the world's most recognized trademarks. In surroundings where such a bright, modern symbol would look out of place, it is adapted. In one historic British site, it is chiseled into a stone fascia.

▶ Restaurants have to be on their best behavior all the time. As well as pre-arranged inspections, a quality assurance team makes frequent unannounced visits.

BUSINESS MATTERS: TRADEMARKS

The Golden Arches sign on its red background is McDonald's trademark, or brand name. A trademark symbolizes a company's reputation. Nobody else may use it or reproduce it without permission. People who copy it or attempt to pass their stores or goods off as McDonald's can be prosecuted. McDonald's is among the ten best-known brands in the world.

McDonald's image

The way a McDonald's looks and operates is an essential part of the company's image – the way it presents itself to the public. Mac and Dick McDonald recognized the importance of this back in the 1950s. Their model restaurant was designed to grab attention. Today McDonald's units are an instantly recognizable feature of main streets and shopping centers. Many are in-store units in department stores. Some are drive-through units where drivers buy their food at a service window and drive on. Some are mobile kiosks that drive to the customers. You will find McDonald's in airports and stations, on trains and ferries, and even in hospitals.

CLEANLINESS AND TLC

"Cleanliness is like a magnet drawing customers to McDonald's," says a company slogan. McDonald's insists that its restaurants and staff are spotless. Counter staff must look clean and welcoming. They must serve their customers and treat the food with "tender, loving care." Hosts or hostesses must be ready to help customers at all times, helping them to serve themselves, find a seat and look after their children.

BUSINESS MATTERS: CORPORATE IDENTITY

The way in which a corporation is seen by the general public is known as its corporate identity. Companies work hard to create and preserve a good image. McDonald's wants its customers to carry an impression in their minds of quality, cleanliness, service and value – a restaurant where the whole family can have an enjoyable experience. Market research has shown that the sign of the Golden Arches helps to fix this impression, so that every time they see it customers remember McDonald's as a good place to eat. Advertising and good public relations, especially with the local community, strengthen a company's corporate identity.

◀ One more star to go, Louise sets out salads with a gloved hand and tender loving care.

Conquering the world

Between 1965 – the year in which McDonald's went public – and 1977, the company grew from a medium-sized organization with 700 restaurants in the United States to a giant with 5,000 all over the world.

Financial experts at the start of the 1970s forecast that in the following decade McDonald's would probably make too much profit. If the money was not invested, much of it would go in taxes. It would be better to open more restaurants. But perhaps there were already enough restaurants, at least in the United States.

McDonald's abroad

Elsewhere in the world fast food was almost unknown. McDonald's was the first company to try to export America's love of fast food and change the habits of other nations. After a shaky start in the late 1960s, McDonald's went on to conquer country after country. Golden Arches greet the visitor to cities as far apart as Tipperary and Tokyo. In Japan and the Far East beef has become popular with people brought up on a diet of fish and rice.

▲ Ray Kroc and Fred Turner parade their commitment to cleanliness at the opening of McDonald's 2,500th restaurant.

SELLING AMERICA

In 1990 McDonald's opened its first restaurant in Moscow. It was a symbol of American freedom and commercialism in a country that knew little of either. In 1991 the Soviet Union broke up. Price controls ended in 1992 and so prices rose. The price of a hamburger and French fries was now as much as some people earned in a month. But those

◄ Life has been hard for the Russians since the break-up of the Soviet Union. Few people can afford a burger at the Moscow McDonald's, but there is no doubting that the vast majority of Russians would like one.

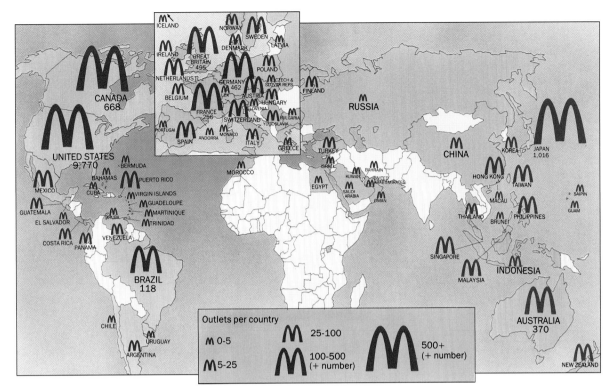

Outlets per country

M	0-5
M	5-25
M	25-100
M	100-500 (+ number)
M	500+ (+ number)

▲ The map shows the march of the Golden Arches across the face of the world.

Local control

McDonald's uses the same franchise system overseas as in the United States. In each country where it operates a local entrepreneur serves as McDonald's manager. This person, in consultation with McDonald's in Chicago, organizes the building of restaurants, the selling of franchises, the search for satisfactory suppliers, the setting of prices, and the organization of local advertising and promotions.

who could afford to, still lined up for a taste of the western way of life.

The Moscow restaurant is managed and supplied from McDonald's Canada – the quality of local beef could not be guaranteed. The restaurant is not profitable, but it is good for McDonald's image and has attracted worldwide publicity. The same is true of McDonald's 11,344th restaurant. This was opened in China on October 8, 1990. It is owned by McDonald's Hong Kong but managed by the Chinese.

BUSINESS MATTERS: MULTINATIONALS

Multinational companies operate in several countries. Often these companies are very powerful. It benefits them to set up companies in countries poorer than their own. Labor and raw materials are cheaper, taxes are lower and they avoid import tariffs. Most countries welcome multinationals because they provide employment and tax revenues and create a demand for other services and raw materials. Critics, however, say that they have too much power, that they exploit poor nations by taking back home the profits that the local community has helped to create. This is not the case, however, with McDonald's.

Hot competition

The fast-food industry is one in which many companies compete for customers. In the United States alone, fast-food sales amount to more than $200 billion. During the 1980s, business was good and McDonald's and other food chains increased their sales steadily. But there has been a recession during the 1990s and the rate of growth of the market has slowed. During a recession businesses try to cut costs and lower prices to increase their share of a decreasing market.

Price wars

In the United States McDonald's has two main rivals, Burger King and Wendy's. They of course use the same tactics to attract more customers, and the result is a continuing price war. A California company called Taco Bell, owned by PepsiCo, selling spicy Mexican snacks, reduced its prices dramatically and opened up outlets in airports, schools and colleges, theaters and sports stadiums. McDonald's, unable to reduce prices further without reducing quality, responded by opening airport branches and doing a deal with United Airlines to offer in-flight McDonald's meals. It also opened restaurants in Wal-Mart stores, taking over that company's existing snack bars.

▲ Pizzas and tacos are popular take-out foods. More and more fast-food chains are competing with McDonald's.

BUSINESS MATTERS: RECESSION AND BOOM

Recession is a period during which a nation's business declines. Fewer goods are bought and sold. As a result there are fewer jobs and unemployment increases. With many people out of work, even fewer goods are sold. Businesses use any means they can to increase their sales. If they cannot, they may go bankrupt. During boom times, people have more money to spend. Business is good because companies can sell their products.

▶ Burger King keeps McDonald's on its toes. It operates in all 50 US states and in 51 countries, serving the equivalent of the US population once every three weeks.

BUSINESS MATTERS: GO ONE BETTER

When there are many restaurants or retailers to choose from, all with a similar product or service, why should a customer select one company rather than another? The preferred organization must provide a better product, give better value for money, provide a superior service, and be better at distributing and selling its goods or services, or at making them known through advertising and publicity. McDonald's is good at all these things which is why it can usually go one better than its rivals.

BUSINESS MATTERS: MARKET RESEARCH

Knowing what your customers want and how much they are willing to spend on a product is so important that businesses spend a lot of money researching the market. Many employ special research teams to test products. They get customers to taste new products and answer questionnaires about them. They also test their advertising on focus groups so that they know what will appeal to their target markets. Companies also try hard to find out in advance what their competitors are doing. It is against the law for companies to team up and fix prices, so rival companies try to keep their policies secret.

Changing tastes

Outside of the United States, competition is less fierce, though chains like KFC are opening up outlets alongside McDonald's in many places. Because the popularity of chicken is increasing and that of beef declining, McDonald's has added more chicken and non-beef items to its menu. In the UK, the only traditional take-out food was fish and chips, but as more and more McDonald's open up, more and more fish and chip shops close.

Cultural differences

It is not just fast-food competitors that McDonald's has to compete with. Fast-food itself has little appeal to many western Europeans, especially those of the older generation who think that meals are too serious to be taken out. In Italy, France and other non-English speaking parts of Europe, McDonald's appeal is mostly to teenagers. In some countries, such as India, where the Hindu population regards cows as sacred, McDonald's faces an even greater challenge.

▲ KFC's new roasted chicken products, marketed as Colonel's Rotisserie Gold, are high-value items suitable for family meals.

The people

Almost a million people work for McDonald's directly or indirectly. Many young people get their first job at the local McDonald's. Some stay no longer than a few months. Others hope to make a career with McDonald's.

Like workers on an assembly line, McDonald's kitchen crews perform simple, repetitive tasks that are easy to learn. During busy periods, the food is cooked and served at incredible speeds, so a full day at McDonald's involves periods of hard, hectic work.

Training and careers

McDonald's employs local people in their own communities. It is an equal opportunity employer, and women and people from ethnic minorities are represented at all levels. There are two starting levels: crew member or trainee manager. Crew members can work either full-time or part-time and are paid an hourly rate.

Young people accepted for a position in McDonald's career program can quickly climb the promotional ladder. Trainee managers receive a salary and go through a series of training

▲ Crew members receive stars to denote their level of attainment. Full-time staff are fully trained in five months, part-time staff in ten.

BUSINESS MATTERS: HUMAN RESOURCES

The people who work for a company are its most important investment and asset. It is important to retain talented staff and staff who have become skilled through training. Apart from good rates of pay, companies try to provide good working conditions and incentives. McDonald's gives its crews performance stars on their uniforms, prizes for record sales, bonuses, recognition for outstanding achievements and good career prospects. Managers receive additional benefits, including bonuses, sabbatical leave, increasingly long annual vacations, health care, pension plans, profit sharing and so on.

▶ Learning how to operate and clean equipment like this milkshake machine is part of food hygiene training.

▲ On-the-job training covers food preparation, cooking, serving, cleaning and interpersonal skills.

courses at centers set up in their own countries. They receive even more important on-the-job training at a McDonald's restaurant. If they perform well, they can expect to be running their own McDonald's restaurant a few years after joining the company. There are also many opportunities in support departments and in restaurant development.

Open door

An open door policy allows staff access to managers from the chairman down. Everyone is welcome to make suggestions or complaints. McDonald's also holds frequent meetings called rap sessions where staff can voice their complaints to someone from headquarters or air grievances to a member of management from another restaurant.

▲ Students at Hamburger University take their studies seriously. Giving their training center such a grandiose title was a way of telling the world how seriously the company regarded staff training.

How McDonald's manages

▲ Michael Quinlan is the current chairman and chief executive of McDonald's. He worked his way up through the business from the mail room to the top.

▶ Trainee managers undertake a residential training course as well as on-the-job experience in restaurants.

FRED TURNER, 1932-

Born in 1932, Fred Turner gave up medical studies and spent two years in the US Army before joining McDonald's. He worked briefly at Ray Kroc's Des Plaines restaurant and later as assistant manager at a Chicago branch. In 1956, Kroc hired him to help train McDonald's franchisees and develop the company's operations department. In 1967 he became president of the company and supervised its expansion at home and overseas. Turner succeeded Kroc as chairman of McDonald's in 1977.

Like all major companies, McDonald's has a board of directors. It has a senior chairman (currently Fred Turner) and a chairman and chief executive (currently Michael Quinlan). Together with the other directors, they oversee the work of the company's five vast departments: operational, technical, real estate, financial and marketing. McDonald's USA and McDonald's International form separate divisions of the company.

For management purposes, the United States is divided into regions, each under a regional manager. He or she heads a chain of command down to local senior supervisors and supervisors, restaurant managers and assistant managers. The regional structure is similar in other countries.

In its early days, McDonald's took pride in not having a rigid company structure, complete with organizational charts showing lines of command and levels of achievement. The company fostered a family feeling with family loyalties and family quarrels. The flexible structure allowed ideas to be freely exchanged between departments, especially between operational and technical people.

Open access
Although McDonald's now has a bureaucracy, senior staff are not treated with the awe they command in some companies. Even the chairman is approachable. The staff and the public have open access to him through the company's open door policy. Senior executives are well paid but they do not have especially grand offices or cars.

BUSINESS MATTERS: DIRECTORS AND MANAGERS

Most of the board of directors have senior jobs in the company, overseeing different divisions. These are the executive directors. The board also includes non-executive directors, who do not work for the company. They help the board make decisions and look after the interests of the shareholders. Their role is important. They can criticize members of the board, or even the chairman, without fear of losing their jobs. Most non-executive directors are directors of other important companies.

Managers do not just boss other people about. At every level of a company people have to carry out their jobs efficiently. Managers have the task of seeing that they do. They take charge of, or administer, people and projects. They see that things are done on time and in ways that do not cost the company too much money. Skillful managers do this by motivating their staff to work as hard as possible, so that they can earn more and reach their full potential – or effectiveness – at work. McDonald's managers are encouraged "to do whatever it takes" to give service to their customers. They do not stick robotically to the rule book. They should think for themselves.

▲ A winning team! Together the management and staff of this restaurant have won an award for helping the environment.

NO BEARDS

Ray Kroc disliked people who conformed. He wanted managers with their own ideas, who would not always agree with each other or with him. At the same time he was fanatical about tidiness and correct dress. Neatness and cleanliness were obligatory. He even objected to staff growing beards. Few employees feel obliged to follow his more eccentric rules today, though every manager, like every crew member, learns the importance of personal grooming.

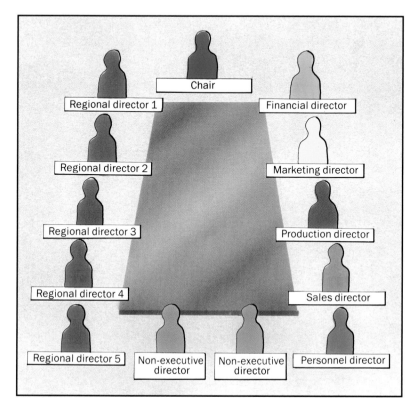

Chair

Regional director 1

Financial director

Regional director 2

Marketing director

Regional director 3

Production director

Regional director 4

Sales director

Regional director 5

Non-executive director

Non-executive director

Personnel director

◀ A typical board of directors of a large company. In smaller companies directors may have more than one role. In very small companies there may be only one director.

In the marketplace

Advertising is one of McDonald's strengths. In the early 1950s, Mac and Dick McDonald used to advertise their success by flashing a neon sign outside the San Bernardino drive-in, saying "Over 1 million sold." In time McDonald's was able to impress the public by saying how many times the hamburgers the company sold would stretch to the moon.

McDonald's did some limited advertising on television in the late 1950s, the first restaurant chain to do so. Because it had no advertising experts, its commercials were not very effective. Franchisees relied mainly on word of mouth and point-of-sale displays to get people into their restaurants.

Television advertising

Since the mid-1960s, nearly all of McDonald's advertising has been on television. In the mid-1980s, McDonald's was spending $180 million on national television commercials in the United States. McDonald's marketing department and its national advertising agency produce the commercials seen on United States television. All the corporations abroad also spend large amounts on television advertising, angling their commercials to suit national markets. In Britain, most advertisements give viewers the prospect of a family treat, good food and good value. They promote special offers and giveaways for children.

▲ There is nothing as bright as a McDonald's welcome. This drive-in can be seen for miles.

FOLLOWING THE FRANCHISEES

During the 1960s, groups of franchisees banded together to buy advertising spots on local television, each paying a percentage of their takings. They also sponsored children's programs because children were their main target market. Local advertising worked. In 1965, McDonald's took a three-minute advertising spot on network television, which meant that its commercial was seen nationwide. Sales rose. In 1966 McDonald's asked its franchisees to contribute one per cent of their takings to fund national advertising. They agreed and the following year set up an organization to control the fund.

▶ This promotion attracted customers by giving them a chance to win a big cash prize.

Tastes of the Orient

6 Mini Vegetable Spring Rolls £1.33   Oriental McRib £1.49
6 Chicken McNuggets Shanghai £1.33 · Toffee and Banana Pie 56p

▲ This promotion showed customers that they did not need to go to a Chinese restaurant to enjoy Chinese food.

▶ Some of McDonald's simplest advertising has been its most effective.

▶ McDonald's cheerful, colorful clown is an effective symbol and spokesperson for the company. He is almost as familiar to American children as Mickey Mouse.

BUSINESS MATTERS: MARKETING

Marketing is the whole process by which goods get from producers to buyers. More people work in marketing than in production. Marketing involves:

market research – seeing who wants what kind of product at what price

product development – making the product right for its market

distribution – getting goods from the producers to the retailers – in McDonald's case the restaurants

pricing – setting the right price, one that enables the company to meet the demand for the product at a price that customers will pay and still leave a profit

promotion – dressing the product, advertising nationally, locally and at point of sale, selling, organizing promotions and after sales service.

▲ McDonald's provides detailed nutrition information on all its products and encourages staff to understand the principles of healthy eating.

▶ As fast as trash (not just McDonald's) builds up in the vicinity of its restaurants, McDonald's staff are out to collect it.

McDonald's and its public

How McDonald's looks in the eyes of its potential customers and investors is of vital importance to the whole company. Every effort is made to present McDonald's as a caring company offering wholesome food and a happy eating experience to the public. Its communications department keeps the media up to date with company developments, presents positive stories in the form of press releases, answers criticisms and copes with controversies. It produces leaflets for its customers that explain about nutrition and the environment. It counters negative publicity from environmental and health pressure groups. It organizes sponsorships, educational programs, and other charitable activities, all of which present McDonald's in a good light.

McDonald's and the environment

The packaging that McDonald's uses is cost-effective and convenient, but when not disposed of properly, it can become litter. McDonald's aims to be a good neighbor. It encourages tidiness by placing trash cans outside its stores and sending out litter patrols to clear up after people who persist in strewing the streets with used packaging. In the UK it works with the Tidy Britain Group and organizes litter-related competitions for schoolchildren.

CFCs

The packaging itself caused McDonald's and the community concern in the late 1980s. Until 1988 hamburgers were sold in cartons made from plastic foam. The process of making the foam was one source of chlorofluorocarbons (CFCs), chemicals harmful to the ozone layer of the atmosphere. Now the packaging is CFC-free. CFCs are also used in refrigerators and other electrical equipment, which the company is gradually phasing out.

Cutting waste

Waste reduction and the re-use of materials are also a concern of McDonald's. Wherever possible they use materials that can be recycled. Waste packaging is sold for charity and waste cooking oil is sold to be made into animal feed and other products. The money is given to charity.

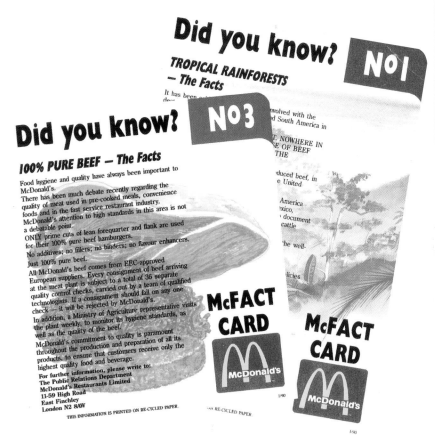

▲ To counter adverse publicity, McDonald's makes leaflets available in all its restaurants stating the facts about its products and policies.

RAINFORESTS

People all over the world are concerned about the survival of rainforests. In the past much forest was cleared to make pasture for cattle. As a result, conservationists have attacked McDonald's. McDonald's insists that it uses only domestic beef in the United States, and that it requires proof from its suppliers in South and Central America that their beef comes only from cattle reared on long-established ranches. Despite this, some people still claim that McDonald's is responsible for the popularity of all hamburgers and therefore for any rainforest that has been cleared to raise cattle for other companies' hamburgers.

BSE

The appearance of the brain disease BSE (bovine spongiform encephalitis) in cattle during the late 1980s and early 1990s affected sales in many fast-food chains and supermarkets in Britain. McDonald's responded quickly by publicizing the fact that brains (the part thought to pass on BSE) are not used in their hamburgers. Even so, people were scared to eat ground beef for a time and sales suffered.

Profits for a good cause

As it has grown and expanded since the late 1960s, McDonald's has been consistently profitable. It invests much of its profit in extending its own business, but also sets aside millions of dollars each year to fund charitable activities. In the United States McDonald's and its franchisees donate more money to registered charities than any other commercial enterprise. The restaurants also raise money for charities, especially for Ronald McDonald Houses.

All McDonald's managers are expected by the company to support local charities, especially children's ones. Charitable works in the community vary from restaurant to restaurant but range from parties for disadvantaged children to coffee mornings for mothers. These activities are not just good for the community. They provide good publicity for McDonald's and enhance their corporate image.

▲ McDonald's sponsorship of the 1994 World Cup, played in the United States, meant that its name was in front of the cameras at all the matches and beamed into homes around the world.

GOOD WORKS

National programs:

* Ronald McDonald Children's Charities donate money to child welfare causes.
* Ronald McDonald House program aids more than 2,500 families every night, providing 163 homes-away-from-home in 12 countries
* sponsorship of World Cup 1994
* sponsorship of major athletics teams and events
* sponsorship of McDonald's Child of Achievement Award for children of special courage or kindness
* sponsorship of Waste Reduction Action in partnership with the

▲ Princess Diana's involvement with the Child of Achievement program guarantees extensive media coverage for McDonald's.

Environmental Defense Fund
* supports the American Red Cross, providing relief to thousands of families affected by floods, hurricanes and earthquakes

Ronald McDonald Houses

Ronald McDonald Houses are located next to hospitals. They provide accommodation for the families of seriously ill children who have to spend a long time in the hospital. The children can stay there too if they are well enough.

The idea for the houses came from an advertising agency used by McDonald's franchisees in Philadelphia. The agency heard of an appeal from Fred Hill, a local American football star. Hill, whose daughter Kim was in the hospital with leukemia, was trying to raise funds to build a home away from home for families with children in the hospital. Many parents had problems visiting their children because they lived a long way away and could not afford a nearby hotel room. Local McDonald's franchisees responded by raising $50,000 for the first Ronald McDonald House, which opened in Philadelphia in 1974. Today there are more than 160 Ronald McDonald Houses throughout the world.

* higher education scholarships
* school teacher and governor support programs
* resource packs for children and teachers

▼ Even without media attention, Ronald McDonald is there to cheer up children in hospital.

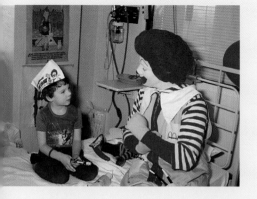

Local activities:

* education awards to employees to cover fees and books
* parties for children with special needs
* visits to local hospitals by Ronald McDonald
* "litter contests" between local youth groups
* loans of "orange-bowl" orange-drink dispensers for use by fundraising organizations
* road safety campaigns
* painting and craft competitions with achievement certificates for local schools
* training for unemployed people
* coffee mornings for mothers' groups and senior citizens

▶ Mobile units like this one take McDonald's to sporting events.

The future

In November 1984, some 10 months after the death of Ray Kroc, the 50 billionth hamburger was served to Dick McDonald at a celebration in New York. Many asked "Will McDonald's go on to serve another 50 billion?" The question is not easy to answer.

Too many McDonald's?

Some people say that there are too many McDonald's. In some places in the United States there are only two streets between two McDonald's restaurants, which was one reason why McDonald's chose to expand abroad and will continue to do so. To increase its profitability in new markets, more and more restaurants need to be introduced so that McDonald's can benefit from economies of scale.

▶ Drive-ins like this one enable busy people to pick up the family supper on their way home from work.

On the move

Public tastes change. McDonald's has always been quick to change its operation and image to suit these changing tastes. Drive-ins went out, sit-down or take-out stores came in. Now, with an even more mobile population, drive-through restaurants are popular again. McDonald's is also on the move, using mobile kiosks that can be driven to sporting events, putting restaurants on trains, and building new restaurants at highway service stations. McDonald's will go where the people go, even if they have to build restaurants in space.

Time for change

Products have changed, too, to meet changing tastes. McDonald's has always relied heavily on beef, but now more and more people are showing a preference for white meat and fish. To meet this need, McDonald's has added new products to the menu and will continue to do so. But this will make the menu ever larger, and so some less well-loved items will be phased out.

McDonald's knows that it must change more than its menu to stop itself from slowing down. However successful a product or an organization is, customers and employees always need a change. McDonald's does not plan big changes to what is a winning formula, but it will continue to improve products and equipment, and create new and exciting restaurants around the world.

> **BUSINESS MATTERS: ALL CHANGE**
>
> Nothing in business ever stands still. If your business stands still, you can be sure that your competitors' will not. So good managers and business people look to the future. They know that their business is only as good as its people, their skills and its equipment. Technology changes at an amazing speed and so do public tastes. Unless businesses keep up with changes and get ahead, they can be outstripped by their rivals.

▼ Making changes requires confidence, caution and courage, but McDonald's has often changed to meet challenges. Who knows? One day it may have to set up in space.

Create your own business

McDonald's makes money by giving its customers quality, service, cleanliness and value. Can you and your friends do the same? Can you think of a product or service to sell? Suppose you set up a car-washing service, using your school logo as your trademark. Before you start, get permission from your school and your parents.

Management
Select a small team of managers, one to buy materials, one to manage the money, one to handle publicity and so on.

Capital
If everyone contributes some of their own money, they may find their parents more willing to lend some. You must return investors' money with interest.

Planning
Find out about your customers. Where are there most cars? Who will employ you? How much will they pay? How much does the competition charge? Do some research. Ask your parents and their friends. Estimate the time it takes to clean a car, and the best way to do it. How many people do you need? What materials? Where will you get your water? Are you covered by insurance? You may need advice from an expert.

Presentation
In this business you and your hard work will be the product, so make sure your

Look smart and identifiable. Give quality, service, cleanliness and value. The faster you go, the more money you will make.

work is of the highest quality. Find out what your customers want – when, where and how they want their cars cleaned – and give it to them.

Identify yourselves with a smart, simple uniform, such as clean jeans and a T-shirt with your logo on it. Be cheerful and polite. Devise a standard, distinctive way of carrying your equipment – cloths, sponges, soap, wax, bucket – so that each item serves its purpose and is part of your image.

◀ Plan your business carefully. Remember you need capital, people, equipment and marketing.

▼ Proper businesses present their figures as a profit and loss account like this.

PROFIT AND LOSS ACCOUNT		
Income		300.00
Less Cost of Sales		
Cleaning equipment	20.00	
Liquids and wax	10.00	
Leaflets	10.00	
Uniforms	60.00	
	100.00	(100.00)
Gross profit		200.00
Less Overhead		
Wages	10.00	
Stationery	5.00	
Telephone	5.00	
Bus fares	3.00	
	23.00	(23.00)
Net profit		177.00
Loan repayment	100.00	
Interest	10.00	
	110.00	(110.00)
Net profit after interest		67.00

Cost

Do some math. How much will you have to pay for T-shirts (and laundry) and cleaning materials (bought in bulk)? How much will it cost you to advertise and sell your service? Remember your overhead, items like telephone calls, bus fares and stationery.

Add up all the costs. Work out how many cars you have to clean to cover your costs and get back all the money you have spent. Work out the profit per car cleaned.

Work out when you will spend money and when you will make it. Do a cash flow forecast of money in and money out. It is no use getting money tomorrow if you need to buy more polish today.

Selling

Get local shops to put up posters for you, hand out leaflets at stores or tuck them under windshield wipers. Drum up publicity. Ask the local paper to run a story. Send them a photograph of the "Clean Car Team." Get your parents to tell their friends.

Service

Give everyone in the team a specific job – washing, rinsing, waxing, preparing bills, collecting cash, inspecting the finished job. You can each do different jobs on different days, so that you don't get bored. Work out the best system. Remember that the quicker your service is, the more money you will make.

Profit and loss

Keep a record of what you spend and receive. Continually analyze your performance. Can you make savings of costs and time to increase your profit?

Decide what to do with the profit you make. Will you give some to charity, some to your school? Will you reinvest some? Will you license your system? What would Ray Kroc have done?

The language of business

Accounts Records that show money going in or out of a business.

Additives Variety of chemicals, natural and artificial, added to foods to increase their nutritional value or enhance them in some way.

Advertising Making publicly known. Advertisers use television, radio, newspapers and so on to tell everyone how good their product or service is. See also Promotion.

Analyze To examine something minutely.

Assembly line Series of machines and workers in a factory set up to assemble a product in a sequence of tasks.

Assets Anything owned by a business including property, money, goods and machines.

Automation Manufacture of a product using machines rather than people.

Bankrupt Having no money in the bank or any means of paying debts.

Billion A thousand million or, in Britain, a million million. Billions in this book are a thousand million.

Binders Substances added to food to make the particles stick together.

Blueprint Blue photographic print of an architect's or other plan.

Board of directors See Directors.

Brand The name of a company's product. See also Trademark.

BSE A brain disease of cattle. Short for Bovine spongiform encephalopathy.

Bureaucracy Officials who run an organization, and the system of office routines they impose.

Buyout The purchase of shares belonging to owners of a company in order to gain control of it.

Business An organization that sells goods or services.

Capital Money needed to start a business and keep it going.

Carhops Waiters who brought food to customers in their cars in drive-in restaurants.

Cash flow The rate at which money enters and leaves a business during any period of time.

Cent See Dollar.

CFCs Chemicals dangerous to the earth's protective layer of ozone. Short for chlorofluorocarbons.

Chairman The person who leads a committee or board of directors. Also called a chairperson or chair.

Chief executive The highest-ranking person in a company who has full power to act and make

decisions on behalf of the company.

Client Another name for a customer.

Commercial To do with trade, or a television or radio advertisement.

Commercialism Interest in business and making money by trade.

Communications department Public relations department responsible for issuing information about a company and making sure that the company's relations with the general public are good.

Company Organization of a group of people to carry on a business. Companies may be small or large, public or private. See also Corporation.

Competition The struggle for customers and profits between two or more enterprises in the same field.

Contract Legal agreement between two or more persons. It can be written or spoken.

Corporate identity A company's image in the eyes of the public.

Corporation Business corporations are usually large, centrally organized public companies.

Costs The amount of capital that it takes to make and sell a product or service.

Credit To give credit is to allow time for a payment to be made. A creditor is a person or business to whom a business owes money.

Customer Anyone who buys from a seller, especially one who buys regularly.

Directors People who guide the activities of a company and make its most important decisions. They are members of the board of directors, which is led by the chairman or chief executive. They are also called corporate officers.

Distribution The means by which a company's product reaches its customers.

Dividend A small part of a company's profits paid to a shareholder in return for his or her investment.

Diversification The widening of the range of goods and services produced.

Division of labor A system that splits up the production process so that each worker or group of workers carries out a specialized job.

Dollar Unit of US currency made up of 100 cents. The equivalent in UK

pounds at the moment is about 66 pence, but rates of exchange between countries vary all the time.

Earnings Money gained by a person working or by a company selling.

Economy of scale A fall in the cost of production resulting from an increase in the size of a business.

Efficiency The best use of resources and effort to attain an objective.

Entrepreneur An enterprising person who is willing to take risks.

Environment The surroundings in which people, animals and plants live.

Equal opportunity employer A company that hires staff on the basis of their qualifications, regardless of skin color, ethnic background, religion, sex, age or disability.

Executive director A director who works for a company. A non-executive director is a member of the board but is not employed by the company. See also Directors.

Exporting Selling goods abroad.

Fast food Prepared food that is ready to eat or can be quickly made ready by, for instance, reheating.

Fillers Additives used to increase the bulk of processed foods.

Financial director An executive responsible for financial planning, making and receiving payments, and keeping records. Also called a treasurer.

Financial To do with money.

Financial institution A business, such as a bank, savings and loan, or insurance company, that deals in money.

Flavor enhancers Chemicals that bring out the flavor of foodstuffs and make them more succulent.

Focus groups Specially selected discussion groups who assess products and make suggestions.

Franchise A special agreement or license granted by a company.

Franchising agent Person employed by a franchisor to supervise the sale and operation of franchises.

Freehold Land or property owned outright.

Giveaway Small gift given away as a promotional item.

Goods Things produced for sale by a business.

Gross See Net and gross.

Growth Expansion of a business to increase profits.

Human resources The people who work for a business. Also called staff or personnel.

Image How a company is seen by the public.

Importing Buying goods from abroad.

Incentive Payment or privilege given to make workers produce more.

Interest Money paid to investors for use of the money they have lent, or a financial stake in a company.

Invest To put money into a business or buy shares in it. The sum of money invested is called an investment.

Labor A collective name for workers, especially manual workers.

Lease Contract that grants a person or company (the lessee) the right to rent land or a building for a set period.

License Permit that allows, for example, a franchisee (or licensee) to sell the franchisor's (or licensor's) product.

Logo (short for logogram) A sign or symbol that represents a word and is often used as a trademark.

Loss The money that a business loses when it spends more than it earns.

Manager A person who controls or organizes a business or part of it. A person who organizes staff.

Market The total number of buyers and sellers of a product.

Marketing All the activities involved in putting a product on the market, including research and development, distribution and sales, pricing and promotion.

Market research Surveying people's tastes and requirements to assess the demand for a product.

Mass market The majority of the population. Mostly low-priced products sell to the mass market.

Media Newspapers, magazines, television and radio.

Multinational company Large company that operates in several countries.

Net and gross A gross amount is money paid or earned before tax and other contributions have been deducted to leave a net amount.

Non-executive director See Executive director.

Nutrients Something that provides nourishment.

Nutrition Nourishment from food.

Ombudsman An impartial official appointed to settle disputes.

Outlet Shop, restaurant or other place from which goods are sold to the public.

Overhead General costs, such as rent, heating, stationery and so on, that do not relate to a specific operation or item.

Pension plan A method of saving money to provide a retirement income. Often both employers and employees contribute.

Physical resources Things such as buildings, machines and raw materials that a business uses.

Point of sale The place where a sale takes place, usually a shop.

Premises House or building.

Preservatives Substances added to foods to keep them from spoiling.

President The head of a country, or company.

Pressure group A group of people who work to influence a government or company's activities and policies.

Price The amount of money for which something can be bought or sold. Price is usually determined by supply and demand.

Price controls Regulation of prices by government.

Private company A company that is owned by an individual or group of individuals, and whose shares are not traded on the stock exchange. See also Public company.

Product The thing that a business sells. Products can be goods or services.

Profit The difference between what a company earns – its income – and its costs.

Profit-sharing plan The distribution of some of a company's profits to its employees, either as shares or as a bonus (an extra lump sum of money).

Promotion 1 Moving up the employment scale to a better job. 2 Promoting sales by advertising, publicity and other sales incentives.

Public company A business that offers shares of itself for sale to the general public.

Publicity News or information about a company's activities and products.

Quality assurance Process of checking products to make sure they meet legal and company standards of quality and safety.

Raw materials The ingredients needed to make a product.

Real estate Land and buildings.

Recession A time of unfavorable economic conditions when demand for goods is low.

Recycle To use materials again in order to prevent waste.

Retailer Business such as a shop or supermarket that sells goods in small numbers to customers.

Retail property Buildings, such as shops and restaurants, used for selling products direct to the public.

Risk To invest money which may be lost.

Sabbatical leave Extended period of leave over and above an employee's annual entitlement.

Salary Money paid in fixed amounts, usually monthly, to "white-collar" workers.

Security Something, such as a property or shares, that is offered as a pledge against a loan.

Service Providing help rather than goods.

Shareholder A person who owns shares in a company.

Shares Tiny portions of a company's capital value. The price at which shares are bought and sold goes up and down according to the company's success. See also Stock.

Signage Collection of signs.

Site Ground on which a building (or town) stands, will stand or once stood.

Sponsorship Providing money or other assistance for sporting, charitable or cultural events.

Stock A block of shares.

Stock market Exchange where stocks and shares are traded.

Stockholder Person who holds stock.

Suppliers Companies or individuals that manufacture and sell the raw materials required by a usually larger company.

Target market A particular section of the market, such as teenagers or low-paid workers.

Tariff A tax on imported goods.

Tax Money that businesses and individuals have to pay the government from their earnings.

Technology The application of science to industry.

Trademark A name, design, symbol or some distinguishing mark that makes a company or product unique and recognizable.

Treasurer Another name for the financial director or chief accountant of a company. See also Financial director.

Unemployment Lack of jobs. The level of employment rises and unemployment falls when business is generally good. The reverse happens when business is bad.

Vice-president Person responsible to a senior vice-president or to the board of directors for work done by people under his or her supervision.

Index